BUMBL

Mission SUPER HALLOWEEN

written by
Marsha Qualey

illustrated by
Jessica Gibson

raintree
a Capstone company — publishers for children

Raintree is an imprint of Capstone Global Library Limited, a company incorporated in England and Wales having its registered office at 264 Banbury Road, Oxford, OX2 7DY – Registered company number: 6695582

www.raintree.co.uk
myorders@raintree.co.uk

Edited by Helen Cox Cannons
Designed by Aruna Rangarajan
Original illustrations © Capstone Global Library Limited 2020
Illustrated by Jessica Gibson
Production by Kathy McColley
Originated by Capstone Global Library Limited
Printed and bound in India

ISBN 978 1 4747 9046 8

British Library Cataloguing in Publication Data
A full catalogue record for this book is available from the British Library.

CONTENTS

Meet

BEATRICE HONEY FLINN

(aka BUMBLE B.)

Hi, everyone!

I'm Beatrice Honey Flinn, but I prefer to be called Bumble B. You might think that is a strange name, but it makes a lot of sense. Let me explain:

1 My mum is a beekeeper, and my dad is an artist.

2 I tend to bumble a lot (which is a nice way of saying I'm a little clumsy).

3 My dad says I buzz through life with the persistence and confidence of a bee.

You mix all those reasons with a shortened version of Beatrice, and you get Bumble B. See? It all makes sense.

1+2+3=

BUMBLE B.

Mission

SUPER HALLOWEEN

Chapter 1

SUPER COSTUME

"I have an announcement," Bumble B. said. "Are you listening?"

Her mum put down her coffee cup. "Of course," she said.

Her dad set down his book "Always," he said.

"I have a plan for my Halloween costume," Bumble B. said.

"Are you going to be a bee again?" her dad asked.

"Yes, but not just any bee. My mission is to make myself into a Super Bee!" she said as she held out her drawing.

"Well that's just perfect for my little Bumble B.," her mum said.

"It really is. Now, the cape is the most important thing," said Bumble B. "It has to be long so I can do this."

She whipped her arm in front of her face. She looked like a superhero.

"And I'll need a helmet," Bumble B. added. "I'll be buzzing fast through the air."

"I see," said her father as he looked at the drawing.

"Halloween is this Saturday," said her mum. "We don't have much time."

"Let Mission Super Halloween begin!" Bumble B. said.

They gathered two bin bags, a bicycle helmet, tin foil, black tape, yellow ribbon and glue.

Bumble B.'s dad taped the bin bags together for a cape. Bumble B. and her mum made antennae from tin foil for the helmet.

Bumble B. measured and cut pieces of ribbon and tape. She put those on the cape. The tape was sticky. The glue was messy.

"I could do with a little help here!" she said.

When they had finished, Bumble B. ran to her room to put on the costume.

First, she pulled on striped leggings. Next, her favourite yellow shirt and gloves. Then, her fancy purple shorts with stars on them. Finally, the cape, helmet and polka dot boots.

She raced back to her parents, holding the end of the cape over her face.

She opened her arms wide

and shouted, “I’m Super Bee!”

Chapter 2

SUPER BEE

On Saturday, Bumble B. and her parents rode their bikes to the park. The neighbourhood costume parade was about to start.

"Hurry! Hurry! Hurry!" Bumble B. said.

Her father tied her cape.

“I can see my friends!” she shouted. She started to run but tripped on her long cape.

Bumble B. got up, grabbed her cape and tried again. This time she made it without tripping.

“You all look amazing!” Bumble B. said.

Rosa was a doctor. Kayla was a dancer. Vincent was a fish.

"I see you are a bee – again," Vincent said.

"Wrong!" said Bumble B. She whipped her cape up to her face.

"I'm Super Bee!" Bumble B. said.

"A Super Bee? What's your superpower?" Vincent asked.

Bumble B. didn't have an answer.

"Maybe you make honey super fast," Kayla said.

“Or maybe you sting extra hard,” Rosa said.

Bumble B. made a face. What was her superpower?

The parade music began. Bumble B. let her cape drop to the ground. She started spinning and buzzed loudly.

Behind her, Rosa stepped on her cape. Bumble B. stumbled to her knees.

"I'm so sorry!" Rosa said.

"That's okay," Bumble B. said. "This isn't the first time my cape has been less than super."

"You're not a Super Bee. You're just boring old Bumble B. Flinn," Vincent said.

Bumble B. got up, dusted off her cape and straightened her helmet.

"I'm anything but boring," she said. Then she held her head high as she joined the parade.

Chapter 3

SUPER CAPE

Even without a superpower, Bumble B. was ready to go trick-or-treating. Sweets always made her feel super.

She went with Rosa, Rosa's mum and Rosa's twin sister and brother.

Rosa's mum asked, "What kind of bee are you this year?"

"I'm Super Bee," Bumble B. said. "Let me show you."

She ran ahead, the cape flowing behind her. She made a quick turn to fly back to her friends. The cape got stuck on the neighbour's fence.

Bumble B. stopped in her tracks. "I'm stuck! Help!"

Rosa and

her mum

pulled the cape free.

“Why don’t you just carry the cape over your arm?” asked Rosa’s mum.

Bumble B. didn’t feel super at all. As they went from house to house, clouds rolled in. The sky got darker and darker. Then came a boom, a flash and lots of rain.

"We need to get out of this rain," said Rosa's mum.

"Quick!" said Bumble B. "Everyone under my cape."

Rosa, the twins and their mum got under the cape.

"Good thing I have such a big cape," Bumble B. said. "Let's go!"

They quickly ran to Bumble B.'s house.

"Anyone need a towel?"

asked her dad.

"We're actually pretty dry,"

said Rosa's mum.

"Super Bee saved the day," Rosa said. "It was awesome!"

Bumble B. smiled as they all got out of their costumes. She would have to tell Vincent that Super Bee did have a superpower.

Bumble B. was super at helping her friends. And that was the best power of all!

WRITE ABOUT IT

1. Imagine you are making a superhero costume. Draw a picture of the costume. Write down the superpowers you would have.

2. Pretend you are Bumble B. Write a note in your diary about your fun Halloween.

3. Bumble B. saves the day when it starts to rain. Write a story about a time you helped your friends.

TALK ABOUT IT

1. What is your favourite costume you've worn? Who did you dress up as? Why?

2. Vincent tells Bumble B. that she doesn't have any powers. How does she prove him wrong?

3. Bumble B. has a lot of bumbles throughout the story. Talk about a time you have bumbled. How did you handle it?

GLOSSARY

announcement official statement

antennae feelers on an insect's head

bumble act or speak in a clumsy way

helmet hard hat that protects the head

mission special job or task

neighbourhood small area in a town or city where people live

parade line of people, bands, cars and floats that travels through a town; parades celebrate special events

stumbled tripped

superpower special abilities superheroes have, such as flight or super strength

ABOUT THE AUTHOR

Marsha Qualey is the author of many books for readers young and old. When she's not writing, she likes to read, go for walks by the river, ski in the winter, garden in the summer and play with her cats all year round. Like Bumble B., she has very good friends who make life fun.

ABOUT THE ILLUSTRATOR

Jessica Gibson is a freelance illustrator. With a pen and tablet by her side, Jessica loves creating adorable, whimsical and quirky illustrations, ready to brighten everyone's hearts.